John Safer

To

Jane

and

Charles

John Safer

Frank Getlein

JOHN SAFER

Joseph J. Binns—publisher   Washington, D.C.

Copyright © 1982 by Frank Getlein

All rights reserved, including the right to reproduce this book, or parts thereof, in any form, except for the inclusion of brief quotations in a review

Library of Congress Catalog Card Number 82–90372

ISBN 0–89674–008–0

All photographs in this book are by Judith Goodman and Yoichi Okamoto

I met John Safer in the early 1960's in Washington, D.C. He was a Trustee and I was the newly appointed Director of the Washington Gallery of Modern Art. Though it was evident that his principal motivation was his love of art, John took a warm interest in both the legal and the financial problems of the young museum. One of his fellow trustees, Katherine Graham of the *Washington Post,* had given us a climate control system. It was typical of John's multifaceted personality that he supervised its installation. When a neighboring homeowner tried to enjoin its operation, John was the first to come to our aid, and helped defend us in the teapot tempest that followed (which included the criminal prosecution of the Director). Our mutual endeavors on behalf of the museum helped develop a cameraderie which grew into a friendship that has endured through the years, despite my relocation to the West Coast and then to Milwaukee.

Over the last fifteen years I have visited John's studios, attended his exhibitions and written about his work with a continually growing admiration for its remarkable quality as well as the intensity of his dedication. His early work was inspired by the wonder he found in clear acrylic plastic. Moved by the cleanness, purity, and light responsiveness of that material, he was prompted to assess its reflective, refractive, and light-transmitting properties. His most important show in that direction was held in 1971 at The American Embassy in London under the sponsorship of the Ambassador, the noted collector, Walter Annenberg. His work had divided into two streams—the geometric and the curvilinear-biomorphic. Substantial achievements were attained in both areas; his geometric exercises seemed to stimulate his inspiration in the biomorphic direction.

By the middle 70's John Safer had come to work in brass and bronze, but still maintained his love affair with the clear or smoky acrylic. By 1975 and his Findlay Galleries show in New York, I wrote:

"John Safer began as a constructivist sculptor whose art dissociated itself from natural phenomena in order to create a new reality. Constructivism aspires to an art of absolute form. It is important, in examining Safer's work of this genre, to see not only the highly finished and machined forms, but the emotional content beneath. The minimally oriented geometric pieces show a precision and intelligence which give them an undeniable authenticity . . . These works operate through the dynamism of the interrelationship of their masses and planes, the disposition of space and the esthetic tension established by the sculptor."*

As the years passed, John had carried his metal forming impulses into the biomorphic arena that he had originally reserved for the acrylic blocks which he carved and polished with such delicacy. It was in the later 70's that he produced the polished stainless steel sculpture *QUEST* which is a culmination in the development of a form he had worked with for nearly a decade. One casting is on display in the entrance of the U.S. Department of State. Another belongs to and is on continuous exhibition at the Milwaukee Art Museum. This piece was surely the triumph of his work until that time, and ranks as an outstanding piece of twentieth century sculpture. *JUDGMENT,* a massive bronze work installed several years later on the campus of Harvard University, carried forward the same ideas of spatial exploration and is, perhaps, an even greater achievement. *JUDGMENT* and *QUEST* point out the haunting recurrence of certain themes in an artist's work, the unpredictable yet totally valid consistency that pertains to the unfolding of a discrete and original sensibility.

Gerald Nordland
Director
Milwaukee Art Museum
June 7, 1982

* *John Safer,* Findlay Galleries, New York City, 1975.

Three great forms of bronze, larger than life, stand upon the plaza, taking the sun and shadow. There is an air of presentation, of strength, of decision conveyed in the shapes and textures, the positions of the towering bronzes. Young people move past, through, among the forms.

The sculpture is called *JUDGMENT.* It stands on the campus of the Harvard Law School. It is the work of John Safer.

Starting his career as an artist relatively late in life, John Safer began by improvising within two major traditions of classic, twentieth century art: the constructivism of the Russians prior to World War I, and the biomorphism of artists such as Arp and Miro. In addition, Safer had a philosophic empathy with the Bauhaus approach to abstract sculpture. All three of these adventures in modern art he made his own. He then pushed forward into new territory, new uses of materials, new forms, unexplored by such predecessors as Arp and Brancusi, Malevich and Lissitsky, Archipenko and Gabo. Each of these artists produced individual works that bear some relation to the sculpture of John Safer. But these resemblances were only points of departure for Safer's growing inner vision. His complete body of work, at what must be regarded as his present, mid-career status, forms a unity of its own which cannot be satisfactorily related in toto to any of those earlier twentieth century masters. John Safer's work, while it is a logical outgrowth of the entire modern movement in sculpture, is a unique entity, not only in form, but in its emotional content and the quality of response it engenders in the viewer.

Safer began with a new material characteristic of the twentieth century, loosely called plastic, and quickly developed new approaches and techniques. His experiments in this medium brought to his work a greater variety of form and a greater use of the inherent properties of acrylic plastic than had previously been achieved in modern art.

John Safer began with a visual language utilizing variations on Cézanne's forms, the fluid figures of Arp and Miró, the magnificent surfaces and soaring grace of Brancusi. He then combined those influences and channeled them into his own personal explorations. Returning thus to the giants of our century, using their work as a foundation, he has developed his own sculptural concepts.

The philosophical constructs underlying Safer's work are in the mainstream of twentieth century classicism. As in the theories of Kandinsky, Safer expresses basic human emotions and thoughts in abstract form. His work is not representational, yet it does represent the human condition. The language of art goes beyond representation, expresses emotion and thought in terms of line, color, mass, movement. It exists in the bison of Lascaux, in the calm confidence of the victors in Velasquez' scene of Breda, in the heartbreaking sorrow of Michelangelo's *Pièta.* The emotional-intellectual content inheres not in the subject but in the manner in which the subject is depicted. So it does in the sculpture of John Safer.

Note

Shortly after the turn of the century, a German chemist invented a new acrylic plastic. This material, polymethyl methacrylate, was as transparent as the finest glass but somewhat softer and more malleable. It was manufactured and marketed under the name of Plexiglas. Later it was licensed to manufacturers in other countries and marketed under a variety of names. Dupont called it Lucite and it was by that name that it became best known throughout the United States. For simplicity's sake throughout this book the material will be referred to as Lucite.

John Safer is that rarest of residents in the Nation's capital, a native born Washing-
tonian. Military service, law school, and a brief career in television took him away from
Washington for about ten years. Then, he returned to become a real estate developer,
and from that, moved into finance. But he was always aware of a bent toward art; and
one way or another he pursued his artistic vision over the years. Finally, twenty years
ago, those impulses came together in sculpture.

An only child in a large household, he grew up feeling he was inept with his hands.
That idea was repeatedly demonstrated to him by his own lack of skill compared to
those around him. Those around him were, of course, adults. Safer was not as dextrous
as his elders, and they were quick to point that out to him. School reinforced this lack
of confidence. Born in 1922, he grew up in a period when fast advancement in school
was automatically regarded as desirable. As a result, he was allowed to speed ahead and
graduate from high school when he was fourteen. Again, he was forced to compare himself
with his fellow students, older and physically more developed. The pattern was effectively
set.

Nonetheless, he wanted to express himself in the field of art. Painting and sculpture
appeared beyond his abilities. Magazines featuring contemporary photography were about
the house. He was attracted on sight to the austere, architectural, and mechanical photos
stemming from the Bauhaus school. He obtained an elementary camera. Following the
concepts he admired, he framed telegraph poles and wires, passages of fence, the open
ends of stacked drainage pipes; but somehow the pictures were not as clean and pure in
print as in his mind's eye. He learned that both skill and craftsmanship are necessary,
and that cleanness and purity can be chimeras far easier to seek than to find. He did,
eventually, turn himself into a highly skilled photographer, complete with the dark room
mastery he had barely heard of as a schoolboy. More important, he realized for the first
time that there was something very satisfying, something he responded to, in the making
of arrangements of shapes in space.

After high school, his parents wanted him to attend Harvard, and he dutifully applied.

Unaware of that university's tradition of accepting the occasional bright student several years younger than most of his classmates, Safer was terrified at the prospect. He solved his problems during the college board examination; he wrote nothing at all during the English test, using the time to think with trepidation about being at Harvard at his age and size.

That solved the Harvard problem. Blank papers rarely produce acceptable grades. He entered George Washington University, in those days a strictly local, almost neighborhood college, not at all the now sprawling, prestigious seat of learning famous for saving the lives of wounded presidents and teaching the law to generations of Capitol Hill people. He was bored and unhappy, and his school work reflected this. At best, he got by. A turning point came with a course in economics. The professor was Edward Acheson, the brother of the Washington lawyer and future Secretary of State, Dean Acheson. One day Professor Acheson gave the class a formula used by banks to calculate how much of their current assets they could legally lend. This formula, the professor explained, made unnecessary the previous, laborious, trial-and-error process of daily calculations; but, he added, neither he nor anyone he knew of, was aware of its derivation. John Safer spent that evening working on the formula and the next day gave Acheson a proof of how the formula was arrived at, why it worked. It was a moment of recognition for the boy, recognition by someone he respected, recognition of relationships between abstract elements which, properly perceived, lead to an equation, a state of dynamic balance. The perception probably figures in Safer's sculpture, but its immediate result was a birth of confidence in his own abilities, and a master-apprentice relationship with Acheson. His undergraduate years took on an interest they had not had before and he became an outstanding student.

Just before graduation, World War II arrived. John Safer enlisted as an aviation cadet. This did a number of things for him, all positive. The ancient derogatory military charge could be made in an entirely positive sense; he found a home in the Army—or the Air Force, as it began calling itself just about then. He had his first experience of "shop", a line of study he had somehow missed in his skewed schooling. Also, he found himself in the company of a group of physically oriented young men, and discovered his own natural abilities in athletics—a very real love of sports that has stayed with him throughout his life. His specialty became communications. This was based on electronics, for which he discovered he had both an aptitude and a taste.

Stationed in India at the war's end, he stayed on in the service for an extra year and was reassigned to Europe. During that year, he was able to travel widely about the Continent. He was stationed in Greece and remembers primarily the Parthenon, the most perfect structure he had ever seen. In Florence, after all the treasures of the Uffizzi and the Pitti flooded his mind, what he remembered most vividly were Ghiberti's bronze doors of the Baptistry and the David in the Academy. Sculpture was making itself felt. It had before. Growing up in Washington, he had laughed at most of the public sculpture in that city of public sculpture, but at an early age he had seen the Saint Gaudens Adams Memorial in Rock Creek Cemetery, popularly called "Grief", and had gone back to it again and again.

At the end of his military service he returned home to Washington where studying law comes as naturally as show business in Hollywood. This time he did gain admission to Harvard, took his law degree and in the process worked on sound and set design for the Brattle Players, learned to know the Museum of Fine Arts and to love the Gardner.

With graduation, he chose communications as his field and found a job with a Cleveland television station. Safer started in Cleveland as a kind of handyman. In three months he was program director. This position led to two formative experiences. The first was developing an evening news program, infusing it with visuals and pacing it, giving it rhythm and movement, and seeing it rise to the top of the heap in Cleveland, ahead of the network competitors. In the same line, he put together a movie program stressing American classics and the English and Continental movies that hadn't yet reached Cleveland. This too was effective and successful. Thus, learning what he could do in television, he also learned the corollary, what he couldn't do.

Estes Kefauver came to town with the Senate hearings on organized crime. Safer saw in the announced hearings a great opportunity for his station to originate a new type of show for national consumption. His station manager resisted, finally expressing his veto with the curt observation, "because I say so and I'm the boss". The Cleveland station didn't cover Kefauver. A month later Kefauver moved his hearings to New York where they were picked up by national television and became the top rated show in the country. John Safer realized that one good way to avoid binding restrictions was not to have to defer to others for key decisions. Although he didn't realize it yet, he was describing the condition of being an artist.

Safer married in Cleveland in 1950 to Susanne Renee Arvay, who had come there at the age of nine with her family, refugees from a Vienna just taken over by Hitler. They had two children, Janine, born in 1955, now Mrs. Jonathan Whitney, and a son, Thomas, born in 1960. John and Susanne were divorced in 1979.

In the midst of all the events in Cleveland television, Susanne Safer strongly encouraged her husband to take up photography seriously. While in Europe, he had acquired a good camera and made one photograph which he felt began to approach his old goals, a picture of the Brandenburg Gate. Now he acquired more cameras, filters, lenses, plus darkroom equipment and began to become a competent photographer. He continued and became very competent indeed. He pursued his photographic work while traveling about the world. Studying a group of the pictures Safer produced during this period, one sees that they are not merely competent, they are works of abstract art. From one point of view they are travel photography, but the pictures are not representations of easily recognized places, they are not the Brandenburg Gate in national variations. They are examples of subtle composition, good color arrangements, attractive subjects revealed at their most intriguing.

Aware that he had the ability to develop good television programming, and aware of the limitations of local television, Safer was thinking of moving on to network TV when he moved, instead, back to Washington. His father became very sick and John Safer was called home to manage the family properties until his father was able to do so again. The young man found that the family properties were elderly and few. Half

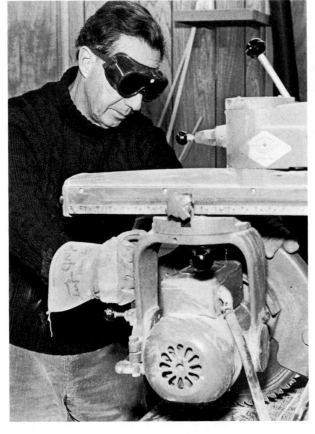

against his will be became interested in their problems. His father did not recover and died shortly after Safer's return to Washington. Safer then set himself the task of transforming the family's holdings into investments which would yield enough income to support his aging relatives with a minimum of personal supervision, so that he could get back to his career in television.

Things did not work out as he had hoped. To achieve his goals, he became more and more involved in real estate trading and developing in the Washington area. As time passed, the investments approached and passed the goals he had set, but at the same time, he became aware that it would be almost impossible for him to withdraw without endangering the structure he had created. He continued. As the years went by it became evident that he would never return to television. At some point, his business, like all businesses beyond a certain level, led to finance. Since he had been educated, after all, in economics, he followed the dictates of the situation. This led to an investment in Financial General Bankshares, a multibank holding company based in Washington. He served there for some years as Chairman of the Executive Committee, and then moved to D.C. National Bank, where he became Chairman of the Board.

The affinity between finance and art is ancient and honorable on both sides. The Florentine Renaissance was underwritten to a very large extent by the Medici, whose family trade was international finance. Earlier still, Giotto executed the frescoes that began it all, the cycle in the Arena Chapel, on commission from the Scrovegni family of money-lenders. More recently, the Morgans, the Mellons and the Thyssen-Bornemiszas have represented the tradition. Of course, this situation is unique in that here, the financier is the artist. John Safer always kept an awareness of these traditions and of the fact that putting together a financial arrangement involving multiple parties, properties and purposes calls for talents and decisions similar to those called into play in creating any original composition. Nevertheless, he remained realistic in his appraisal of the practical values of finance.

While pursuing his career in real estate and finance, he had not abandoned electronics. He continued to design and build electronic equipment, both as an amateur music lover in pursuit of ever finer sound reproduction systems and as a professional, through his involvement in electronic business ventures. In both roles, he continued to hone his skills and build his confidence in his hands.

There is a truism that no artist can be removed from his own times. Like most truisms, it contains a good deal of truth. In 1967, becoming steadily more aware that the Vietnam adventure was dragging the United States into an ever-deepening pit, John Safer was a key factor in persuading Eugene McCarthy to run for the presidency. For a short time he directed the McCarthy campaign. Then, just as his father's illness had changed his life in the early 1950's, his own illness put him out of the campaign for three critical months and, perhaps, changed the campaign's course. Safer still feels that the change in U.S. foreign policy brought about by the McCarthy campaign was, after his art, the most significant act of his life.

Re-established in his home town, successful in his new work, Safer moved into sculpture as a result of several things happening more or less at once. He continued in photography, of course. He also participated in the founding of the important, although relatively short-lived Washington Gallery of Modern Art. In the process of installing the Gallery in one of Washington's great old houses near the Phillips Collection, Safer took on the task of designing the lighting. This meant designing a system capable of properly illuminating paintings and sculpture. The pitfalls in lighting sculpture are that a piece can be washed out by light, or, in contrast, it can be so falsely dramatized that the sculpture becomes secondary to the artful work of the light designer. Grappling with these problems, Safer necessarily familiarized himself with a wide selection of contemporary sculptures. There was, he recalls, "some good, a lot bad, but not what I wanted to see." What would he have liked to see? He didn't know yet.

The next step came by serendipity. Dining with friends amid the South Seas ambience of Trader Vic's restaurant one evening, Safer idly held a swizzle stick over the flame of the Polynesian *pau pau*—hot hors d'oeuvres. The stick bent. The diner discovered that he could manipulate and join these sticks to form little abstract sculptures. The breakthrough had come. He had learned over the years that he had the talent to be a highly skilled electronics technician and mechanic. Now he realized for the first time that he could control shapes and space. But psychological barriers are not so easily overcome.

Several years passed, during which he continued to make more abstract little figures. The next step occurred in his home. His eight year old daughter, Janine, returned from school to hear her father complaining about his inability to achieve certain shapes because of the poor quality of the plastic with which he was working. She said, not unreasonably, "Why don't you get some good plastic." Somehow, that did it. The last psychic block had fallen. Now, for the first time, he could do what he knew he must. The next day, the purchase of some blocks and sheets of Lucite opened a new world of possibilities in transparencies. The rest is history, art history.

Safer began by working the "good plastic" with hand tools. The chess set (Pl.14) for instance, was made entirely by hand, all 32 pieces plus the board itself in its 64 squares and multi-levels. It took vastly longer than most championship tournaments and longer, Safer soon realized, than it had to. Like many an earlier sculptor, both abstract and traditional, he saw that much of his work could be done better and faster with heavy-duty power tools, so he began to acquire them. He set up his first studio in what had been his photographic darkroom in his basement. For heating and forming Lucite, he used the kitchen oven. Later, he rebuilt the old carriage house that adjoined his home in Bethesda, Maryland, a Washington suburb. This gave him the studio that he needed, to create the sculptures that were growing in his mind.

In that studio are the machines of his art. The biggest and probably the most useful is a vertical milling machine. The milling machine developed from the lathe but is much more versatile. It can be set up to do individual tasks, but its greatest strength lies in the area of precise repetition. Safer notes sadly that this has little value to him, since everything he does is a pilot model. When properly set up, the machine can perform cutting operations in minutes that would take hours by hand. (It should be added that the phrase "properly set up" is a little deceiving, since it often takes longer to set up a job for a milling machine than to perform the work.)

More familiar to most people is the band saw. Less versatile than the milling machine, the band saw, like any saw, simply cuts through wood, metal or plastic as directed. Then there are grinding and buffing machines that perform the necessary smoothing and polishing the pieces need after having been cut or milled. These differ in size and in the nature of the abrasive material, so that a wide variety of shaping and finishing operations may be performed.

The heat that began with a can of Sterno in a Polynesian setting, then graduated to the uncertainties of a kitchen oven, is now provided by a large annealing oven. It is large enough for an adult to walk into. A constant temperature is maintained by a system of vents in the inner walls and fans behind the vents, so that a steady flow of hot air passes over and around the work being heated. The heat in the oven renders Lucite soft enough to be bent into curves, warps or twists. Safer does his bending by hand—his hands covered with asbestos gloves—he has a maximum of about three minutes after removing the work from the oven during which he can work the material before it hardens.

It can, of course, be returned to the oven for another attempt but this means starting the forming process over from the beginning.

A good ventilating system is essential to a shop like this, which generates unending dust and shavings. Dust is everywhere. It piles up in great heaps during an extended milling, sawing or buffing operation. Besides those heat-resistant gloves, goggles are usually worn by the sculptor as well as a breathing mask.

And the final, most valuable feature of the shop is John Safer's assistant, Fernando Daza, a native of Bogota, Colombia. Fernando has been Safer's right arm for ten years. Safer says "We have developed a wonderful level of communication. When we start to form a new piece, Fernando seems to sense my mental image, almost without words."

Questions of art aside, John Safer has come a long way from the boy who could do nothing with his hands. He owns and operates a shop full of powerful, complex, and dangerous machines. He makes them do what he wants, and out of his work with them have come some of the outstanding sculptures of this century.

John Safer's sculpture began with a simple twist, and has moved inevitably forward. The main thrust of Safer's work has been, paradoxically, to seek and find classic beauty in the most modern of materials and methods for the making of art. In this sense, he is the descendant of Cézanne and of Cubism. Indeed, some of his work is more overtly cubist, in the most literal sense, than anything Picasso or Braque ever painted. But he is also the descendant of the men who built the Parthenon, which, as it has done to millions, took the young man's breath away when, as a restless Air Force officer with an uncertain future, he first climbed the Acropolis and saw the beauty and felt the power of the just proportions of the certain past.

But it did all begin with the twist Safer put on those thin plastic sticks with the wavering heat of a small flame. Not surprisingly, when he had found more suitable plastic material and mastered the techniques of heating and handling it, he memorialized his early efforts in a small series of twist pieces, done in the last year of the sixties and the first of the seventies.

TWIST 23 (Pl. 1) takes full advantage of Lucite's ability to pick up light and color and play with them. Seen here, on the printed page, *TWIST 23* reminds you of the Futurist Italian paintings just before and during the First World War. The colors are similar and so is the dynamic flow and interplay of curving lines and volumes.

There were some twist pieces in Safer's first exhibition, at the Pyramid Galleries, Washington, 1970, and the Westmoreland County Museum, Greensburg, Pa., in early 1971. In the catalogue essay, Donald Karshan, the print collector, scholar and museum founder, said in part: "Not only (does) light . . . reflect off outer surfaces, but can *refract* . . . *within* the mass; reflecting or ricocheting . . . around, off the *insides* of the objects' planes or facets to create a "sparkle" our eyes had previously seen only in tiny gems. . . . Ambient light, once in the sculpture, takes over. We witness its transmissions becoming an aspect of negative space as it displaces positive mass."

Calling Safer "a precisionist of the first order," Karshan concluded that his works "are more than satisfying minimal or neoconstructivist art—they are prototypes of a new family of transparent and light-conductive sculpture."

TWIST 31 (Pl. 2) and TWIST 38 (Pl. 3) could serve as a demonstration of some of Karshan's thoughts. Although quite different from each other, they are more similar in general disposition than either is like TWIST 23. Yet they are also radically different in that TWIST 31 is transparent, TWIST 38 opaque. In TWIST 38—more properly, on TWIST 38 the light reflects along the curving surfaces, delineating precisely the involuted form of the sculpture. In TWIST 31 the light also reflects along both the exterior and interior surfaces. We perceive both at once and don't, at a glance, quite know which is which. The material is being dematerialized before our eyes, even while the shape is being emphatically delineated in its double set of curving lines.

The two pieces are not, however, simply transparent vis-a-vis opaque. On the contrary, the differences in their forms and in the feelings induced by their forms correspond quite closely with the differences between their respective opacity and transparency. Looked at from certain angles, TWIST 31 has a harboring, husbanding, protective and quiet look. Everything is open and gentle. In spite of the coolness of the Lucite there is a basic warmth in the configuration.

How different TWIST 38. Not nearly so involuted as its companion, this piece coils its strength for the impending two-pronged attack along an upward angle: jet fighters taking off, cannons raised to fire, even sawed-off pikes moving to impale. All of this is presented within the basic grace of the curves, but the aggressive feeling is quite clear in contrast to the other work's gentleness.

One of the two major strains in Safer's work to date has been Constructivism. His version is without benefit of the manifestos and self-consciousness of the Russian Constructivists in the World War I era which in the Soviet Union is viewed primarily as the occasion for what turned out to be the Communist Revolution. One of the most pathetic stories in art history is that of the Russian avant-garde painters and sculptors who hailed the Revolution, naively believing that a revolutionary society, which the Bolsheviks proclaimed, would need and want revolutionary art. In a few locations, the artists actually flourished for a short time, but only until the Soviets found out what they were doing and adopted the theory of socialist-realism, which made art, like so many features of life in the new Russia, exactly what it had been under the czars—only with a new cast of characters.

No relationship between art and politics such as that envisioned by the original Constructivists is part of John Safer's artistic philosophy. But individual works do occur in his production which directly remind the viewer of the antecedants of his art in Constructivism. One is TERMINUS (Pl. 4). The message of the name could hardly be clearer. The original Terminus was the Roman god who presided over boundaries, which were often marked by statues of the god or by busts of him mounted on plinths. From the god, his name comes to be applied to the end of the line for railroads, buses and planes.

The center member of this work stands erect, supporting the two square wings that block progress both to the right and to the left. The brass of which the work is made has a signal or announcement quality as in the Roman trumpets and the sounding brass of scripture.

From the classic industrial age method of travel, the railroad, with its familiar terminus, the piece offers overtones of yardmen signalling the passing locomotive with shapes hoisted into positions agreed upon and known. Not so much beyond as enclosing those meanings suggested by the title, the form itself, the double wings attached to the strong vertical, has a perfect balance that defies the gravity of the brass itself. The luster of the surfaces creates the impression of light and weightlessness, just as transparency had done in Safer's earlier work.

SYMBOL (Pl. 5) is one of John Safer's great statements in his earlier medium, Lucite. He could hardly have chosen a more basic and universal "symbol" than the cross. Universally familiar in the European culture which now pervades almost all of the earth's surface, the cross in one way or another is also found in pre-Christian cultures including Egyptian, Chinese, Indian and Peruvian. The varieties include the pre-Christian Tao cross and the Fylfot cross now better known as the swastika, which was a holy sign or symbol for millennia before it became an unholy one. Since the establishment of Christianity, every conceivable geometric, floral and regal development of the cross form has been devised, used, reused, forgotten and revived to be used again. All of these were based, at one remove or another, on one of the forms reflecting the two basic divisions of the ancient Christian Church, the Greek Cross, with equilateral arms, and the Latin Cross, on which the bottom, or pedal, arm is extended and the top arm shortened.

In *SYMBOL*, Safer goes back to the basics of cross-making. *SYMBOL* is somehow both Greek and Latin at once, thus achieving, in a stroke of art, what the two separated Churches have tried in vain to achieve in centuries of recrimination and rapprochement. The illusion that the two crosses are both present is created by the position of the lateral arms, one higher, one lower, echoing the placement of the wings in *TERMINUS*. But there is more, notably the arm that breaks out of the plane of the cross and comes toward the viewer. Here, in the black mirror-like Lucite, it serves a complex purpose. It creates at once a new reflecting surface and a new surface to be reflected in the plane of the cross form itself. Stately and somber in comparison to many of Safer's Lucite works, *SYMBOL* is a commanding presence and a mysterious one, due at once to the original form of a familiar symbol and to the reflections of reflections the arrangement can create, thoroughly confusing the concept of what is reality, what is not.

Finally, there is the base, the pedestal that is an integral part of the piece. Steeply sloped sides suggest the primeval altar and the related forms we know as the ziggurat—the Tower of Babel, the pyramids of Egypt and Meso-America. It is not, however, the antiquity and universality of these forms that give *SYMBOL* its enduring resonance. It's the other way around. Whatever in John Safer's artistic sensibility brought him to these forms and led him to create, astonishingly, when you think of it, a new combination and variation of them, that same murmur of the heart or stirring of the soul led those remote ancestors of ours in the same way to the same forms. It is difficult to find much of what might be called Freudian in Safer's work, even, as we shall see, in a sculpture named for his daughter. But if ever a work of art deserved the name, *SYMBOL*, surely, is Jungian.

One determined to find Freudian motifs or motives might closely scrutinize *BAUHAUS REMEMBERED* (Pl. 6) with its straight, smooth, erect shaft and the twin, rounded appendages on either side. However, the title hauls the piece firmly out of Vienna, north to Weimar and Dessau and the art-architectural-design school which, along with Constructivism, is Safer's principal 20th century ancestral group. The Bauhaus was, among other things, the most peripatetic school since Aristotle's. Besides originating in the two German cities mentioned, and a brief stay in Berlin, it moved on, in the press of circumstance, namely the Nazis, to America, settling principally in Chicago, where the buildings of the Illinois Institute of Technology are perhaps the supreme Bauhaus achievement, and to Cambridge, Mass., where it flourished while John Safer was in that city taking a law degree at Harvard.

BAUHAUS REMEMBERED, in brass and chrome, is a perfect expression of the spirit of that moveable school: chaste, not decorated, everything carried by the shapes and the material, the elements reduced to a minimum.

This is not true of *INTERPLAY II* (Pl. 7) a related piece, despite the substantial difference in the sizes of the two works. Compared with the twenty inch height of *BAUHAUS REMEMBERED*, *INTERPLAY* is a hardly towering three inches. Yet through the magical world of no-scale produced by photography, the two pieces appear here as the same size. Besides the familiar reducing and equalizing effect of photography, we are confronted here with the inherent gift for monumentality in the sculptural world Safer has created and continues to create as his own. *SYMBOL* is one such implied monument that would be awe-inspiring if enlarged several times beyond its already imposing six feet. *INTERPLAY II*, for all the playfulness in the title and the work, could profit from an expansion of up to a hundredfold.

What the work suggests is a contemporary slab office building adorned with two geometric sculptures on the entrance plazas. What it does is mock the stability of the slab with the posing of the cubes on point, a theme more fully developed in *CUBE ON CUBE* (Pl. 9) and related works.

TIME FRAME (Pl. 8) pushes the slab building motif further. Standing just over six feet, the arrangement of Lucite strips casts its shadows upon itself, member to member. It is a quietly witty embodiment of a concept most of us use without visualization. The work reads up as readily as it reads down. In either direction, time is passing, within its frame. The time passed expands to astonishing heights; the time remaining diminishes toward a frightening vanishing point. For a comparable statement on this theme one would have to go back to Louis MacNeice pre-World War II: "The world piles with ash/From fingers killing time."

The cube is the most stable figure of solid geometry, followed by the equilateral pyramid. Rest it on any side and it stays there. With effort, pry it up and unbalance it and it falls immediately into another equal position of total stability. The sphere is a ball and rolls off in any direction; the cylinder rolls only in two, but like the ball, indefinitely; the cone rolls in circles around its point. The cube stays put.

That's the basic strength of *CUBE ON CUBE* (Pl. 9). There are others. But the first is the destabilization of the supremely stable and its re-stabilization in the most apparently unstable position. Like *INTERPLAY II, CUBE ON CUBE* is a small piece that cries out, or rather, states sonorously and solemnly, its monumentality. Although it stands only fifteen inches high, when you shrink your vision down to the scale of the piece, it becomes a monument. It is so because it is one of the fundamental shapes. Given the unusual juxtaposition of its segments, it becomes a surprise. The pieces that come together to form *CUBE ON CUBE* do more than that. Visually, they serve the reflection-refraction of light that is an integral part of much of Safer's work. With the same light coming from the same angle, the component blocks of the two cubes nevertheless react to the light differently. They also react differently to whatever color is around the piece, making the work a color structure as well as a sculptural one. *CUBE ON CUBE* provokes immediate delight and on reflection a touch of awe. The cube on point doesn't violate nature, it transcends nature, and that's what good art, including the most naturalistic, is all about.

If *CUBE ON CUBE* cries out—or states solemnly—its inherent monumentality, a closely related work, *MULTICUBE V* (Pl. 10) achieves it. Paradoxically, the solid masses of *CUBE ON CUBE* seem in one sense more monumental than the separated "multi-cubes" of the other piece, which, in Lucite and bronze, stands over twelve feet. On close examination, *MULTICUBE* turns out to be *CUBE ON CUBE* restated with the top cube, the one on point, fragmented into 27 small cubes, joined together, and the bottom cube segmented horizontally and likewise joined. Both cubes are "exploding" in a controlled, decorous way.

There is a famous, perhaps the most famous, photograph by Berenice Abbott, taken about 1932, called "New York at Night." It was taken from high up, somewhere near the junction of Broadway and Sixth Avenue. You see those thoroughfares coming together, though you don't see them join. What you really see and are forever dazzled by are the cubes of buildings, double cubes, triple cubes, all pierced by and lighted by the implied cubes of windows. It's one of the great photographs of New York. Without reference to the metropolis, *MULTICUBE* expresses very much the same complex feelings. Cubes within cubes, lights within lights: new reality is born of light and eternal forms.

On view in the lobby of an office building at 2020 K Street, N.W., Washington, *MULTICUBE* suggests in its setting of receding columns one of those great seated Buddhas in temples of India and Tibet, the ultimate in human—and divine—stability.

As a coda or envoi to the exhilarating monumentality of *CUBE ON CUBE* and *MULTI-CUBE,* consider *FOUR SPACE* (Pl. 11) seen at rest and in motion. "The least one can ask of a work of sculpture," said Salvador Dali, "is that it stand still." Dali was talking about Calder and Dali was wrong. Here, this sculpture in motion casts Safer's lot in with Calder, no bad place for any sculptor to be. In repose, the piece exemplifies the balance that is part of all of John Safer's constructivist works. That occult balance becomes even more occult when the suspended members are made to move in turn and do not lose their balance. There is thus perfect stability even in motion. But beyond such engineering notes is the delight of that most stable form, the cube, being made a partner in a kind of carnival game. "What you lose on the swings, you gain on the roundabouts," says the

English barker at the fair. *FOUR SPACE* wins both ways.

SHAMAN (Pl. 12) in brass mounted on marble, is an evocation of one strong Bauhaus strain: man expressed as machine. The ritual solemnity of the figure recalls the Shamanic function of cajolling and controlling demons for the sake of the tribe. There is an ironic link between the primitive animism of the Shamans of Asia and the machine-tooled modernism of the Bauhaus. *SHAMAN* connects Safer's constructivism with his other major form, the fluid verticals of flame.

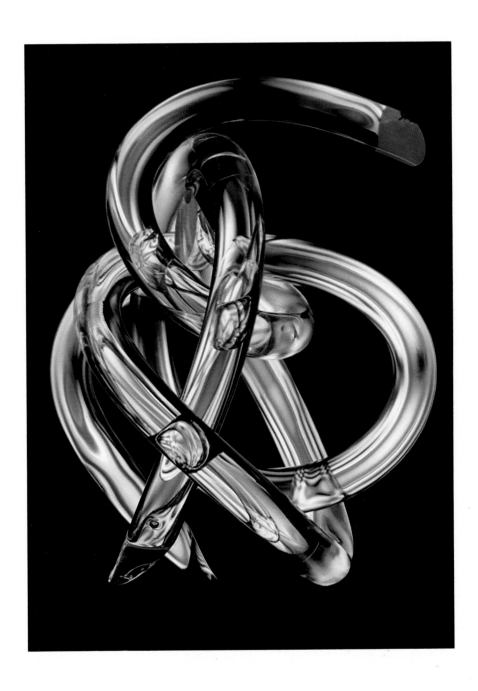

1   Twist 23   *1969   Lucite   18"*   *Mr. and Mrs. Robert Van Roijen, Jr., Palm Beach, Florida*

2   Twist 31   *1969*   *Lucite*   *18"*   *Mrs. Rebecca Safer, Washington, D.C.*

3   Twist 38   *1970*   *Lucite*   *19"*   *Mrs. Susan Safer, Washington, D.C.*

▶

4   Terminus   *1975   Brass   21"   High Museum of Art, Atlanta, Georgia*

5   Symbol   *1970   Lucite   72"*

▶

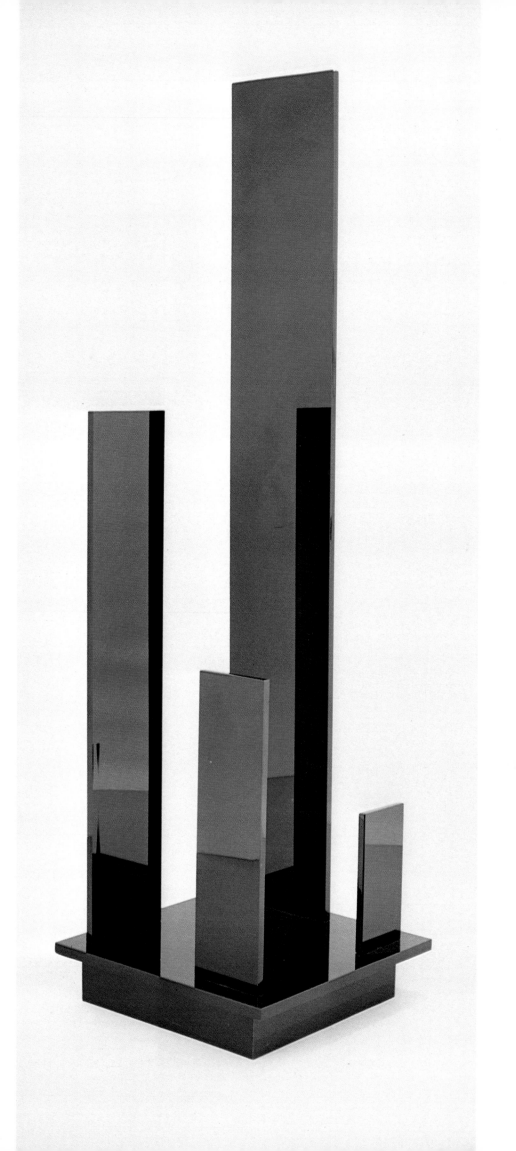

9   Cube on Cube   *1969   Lucite   13"   Philadelphia Museum of Art   San Francisco Museum of Art*

◀   8   Time Frame   *1974   Lucite   74"*

10   *Multicube V*   *1969*   *Lucite and bronze*   *180"*
        Mr. and Mrs. Herbert Blum   *On display in the lobby at 2020 K St., Washington, D.C.*

11   Four Space (*In motion and still*)   *1980*   *Brass, chrome, and marble*   *15"*

12   Shaman   *1979*   *Brass and marble*   *15"*

One obvious note binds together two of John Safer's most formally playful works and his most grave work. The two playful works are so because they are made to play with, a *CHESS SET* (Pl. 14) and a *BACKGAMMON SET* (Pl. 13). The grave work is his most ambitious and fully realized monumental sculpture, *JUDGMENT* (Pl. 20) which stands on the campus of the Harvard Law School, speaking silently to students and faculty of the law they profess and the justice they seek. The common note is that *JUDGMENT* and the two game sets are multifigured, and a second is a shared seriousness. Despite the fact that we "play" chess and backgammon, there is nothing frivolous about these sets of game fields and pieces and, for players, there is nothing frivolous about the activities. As Ingmar Bergman has implied, chess is truly a game of life and death.

Backgammon is even more venerable than chess. A form of it was played in Ur of the Chaldees, which city has given its name to the roots of the whole Mediterranean-European culture. The pieces themselves are simpler than those required for chess. Unlike chess but like life, backgammon is a combination of skill and luck. Chess in theory is a game of pure skill and reason. Critics of American foreign policy have often remarked that we approach that complicated and delicate enterprise out of our national games, football and poker, while the Russians do so out of their national game, chess, with a result, at least in this comparison, to our disadvantage.

The obvious conclusion from that comparison is that Americans should play more chess and it is hard to imagine a greater attraction for playing the game than the set that John Safer has imagined and made.

The set was Safer's first sustained and ambitious piece of sculpture. He carved it by hand, since he had not yet acquired power tools, and it took six months. Seen by itself, as it once was, the set reveals the feeling, the intelligence, the soul of a sculptor. The forms of the chessmen are not playthings. They are embodiments of graduated, measured, differentiated powers. For many centuries, artists have designed chess sets. They were attracted by the game itself, but also by the fact that the chessmen symbolized the power structure of the real world. Those are not dust-smocks the Justices of the Supreme Court wear, nor is it homage to the heavens that decorates our generals with stars. Safer's version of chess combines the democratic and hieratic in much the way that political society does in his native city.

All of the pieces bear a strong family resemblance to one another, more so than do the pieces of the classic chess set most familiar to American players, the Staunton chessmen, and much more so than those of the exotic sets from India, or Medieval and Renaissance Europe. Yet, all the pieces are much more clearly differentiated—and hence practical—than those of many a 20th century chess set undertaken as an exercise in modern design. In clear and dark blue Lucite, the pieces readily explain themselves. The design is essentially contemporary with an occasional look backward, as in the castellation of the rooks, the crown points of the king.

The board is layered and interlocked by transparent cylinders. For the dark squares of the board, Safer used circles, thus relating the ground of the game to the shapes of the pieces. In spite of the transparency and translucency of the pieces, in their squat, compressed shapes there is power waiting to be used and there is a more than faint sense of menace, of implicit threat, of stately danger.

Backgammon resembles checkers in that the pieces are all the same, simple disks of two contrasting colors. Hence the game is an even greater challenge than chess for the artist. Safer rose to the challenge. The path of backgammon is laid out in the traditional fashion, the pieces are gold and chrome. The board is on the same layered principle as the chess board. The combination of the metallic brilliance of the counters and cups, with the classic restraint of the board design, done in black and translucent bronze tones, is exquisite. There is a feeling of superb calculation of color and proportion. It's a good board to play on.

Between those games of free-standing, freely moving pieces, and the monumental *JUDGMENT* at Harvard, there are other moves, just as there are between the King's pawn forward two squares, and checkmate. Another tiny piece, *TANGO* (Pl. 15) all of four inches high, sketches space divided when occupied by more than a single piece. "It takes two to tango", says the song, and that's part of the point here, an important part in terms of the sculptor's development. The tango is also one of the more graceful dances in the ballroom repertoire, embodying sex and drama. Those qualities are implied in the curving forms of the two shapes with their convexitites and concavities, their off-center diagonals within the rectangles of their bases.

Something else altogether is implied in the forms and their relationship in *LINKAGE* (Pl. 16). The sphere is a ball and its companion piece is, among the other features of its shape, a socket. The "linkage" is perfect across the void of space.

SIEGE (Pl. 17) relates very closely to *JUDGMENT*, the major work to date in this group. *SIEGE,* just over a foot in height, is a maquette for a monumental work, as *JUDGMENT* once was. *SIEGE* disposes three forms on a flat space defined by the base. Like *JUDGMENT*, again, *SIEGE* uses its three abstract forms to express a relationship as old as human society. There is, deep in the psyche, a response to the figures shown here. All of us vacillate between the desire to open ourselves to others and the need to withdraw into our private space holding the outside world at bay. Dreams continually grapple with these problems.

With extraordinary economy, John Safer's *SIEGE* encapsulates this most basic human conflict. The tall tower stands, fixed and immobile, in defense, impenetrable in appearance. Against it are ranged the two shorter, more compact, somehow more sinister, attacking forces. They point toward the target, like vicious beasts, like siege guns against the tower. And as we see the inward bulge in the defending wall, our terrors and desires are one, and we know we are confronted with a work of art of immense power.

Things are more mysterious, more evocative than declarative, in *DÉJÀ VU* (Pl. 18), as, of course, things tend to be in that unsettling state. *Déjà Vu* is French for "seen before;" the psychological experience so named is perfectly expressed in the Rodgers-Hart song, "Some things that happen for the first time, seem to be happening again." The three shapes of the small piece have been seen before or will be seen again in Safer's work. Therein lies one meaning of the title. Probably more relevant, these are dream shapes, the kind of stage set in which, in abstract terms, one might well experience *déjà vu*. The shapes, highly individual, are also eternal, the slab, the elongated "y", the curiously Asiatic arch. We have been here before, in the pieces, in John Safer's imaginary world of shapes and spaces and will come again.

TRAJECTORY (Pl. 19) in flowing, curving steel, adds another note to the special vocabulary developed by John Safer. The title is plain enough. The term has meanings in ballistics, missile-science, meteorology, astronomy, as well as golf and tennis, which figure in this body of work. Fire an artillery shell, throw a baseball, flip a coin, and the moving object will follow a path known as its trajectory, a path determined by the force of expulsion against air resistance and sheer gravity. Newton's Second Law allows us to compute trajectory very precisely in time and space and such computations, occult rather than explicit, are implied in much of Safer's work. Here is a trajectory given just a slight touch of torque, a twist, as the broad path leaves its base and narrows after its peak.

Within that complex expression of an abstraction of physics and mechanics, the artist endows the shape with a certain human emotional response. There is a graceful bow, a deference, even a surrender in the trajectory here described, the acceptance of velocity diminished, a flight coming to its finish, ground approaching.

The projectile is seen ascending to apogee and then beginning its descent. It leaves the impression, that were all the mathematics made explicit, the curving, narrowing band would come to a point as the missile approaches impact. Meanwhile, the question is left open. *TRAJECTORY* fascinates by the pleasure it gives the eye as well as by the stimulation of the tactile senses—one feels a part of that curving surface. The strength of this work, as with so much of John Safer's sculpture, lies in those very unanswered questions which cause us to move fractionally closer to an understanding of the time and space of which we, ourselves, are an integral part.

JUDGMENT (Pl. 20) subsumes everything the other multi-unit pieces have achieved and includes more. The three pieces genuinely display three dimensional space. All sculpture is three dimensional, to be sure, but it is possible for three dimensional pieces to be

23

arrayed so as to emphasize only two dimensions. Here the pieces are truly three dimensional and so is their space.

There is nothing overtly suggestive of human figures in the three pieces. Yet they do suggest the theme of judgment. Fourteen feet high and cast in bronze, *JUDGMENT* is by definition monumental. None the less, it has a flowing organic quality. The curves, torques and warps are not "unnatural" to bronze: nothing is. But Safer has mastered that plastic language, that skill of taking a hard unyielding substance and making it appear fluid and organic. The figures stand in the traditional array of forces in Anglo-Saxon and American law: one arguing pro, one arguing con, one in judgment between the two and the two, unavoidably, in constant judgment on the judge.

Like his father before him, Safer has been a non-practicing lawyer ever since he graduated from Harvard and passed the District of Columbia bar examinations. *District Lawyer,* the official journal of the D.C. bar, once asked Safer in an interview, "Didn't training as a lawyer inhibit the spontaneity and intuition . . . essential to your art?" The artist paused, smiled, and answered, "Actually, I didn't attend that many classes."

Perhaps not, but he obviously attended enough to grasp something close to the heart of his unpursued profession. *JUDGMENT,* dated 1979, 30 years after his graduation, was the gift to the law school from his class, that of 1949.

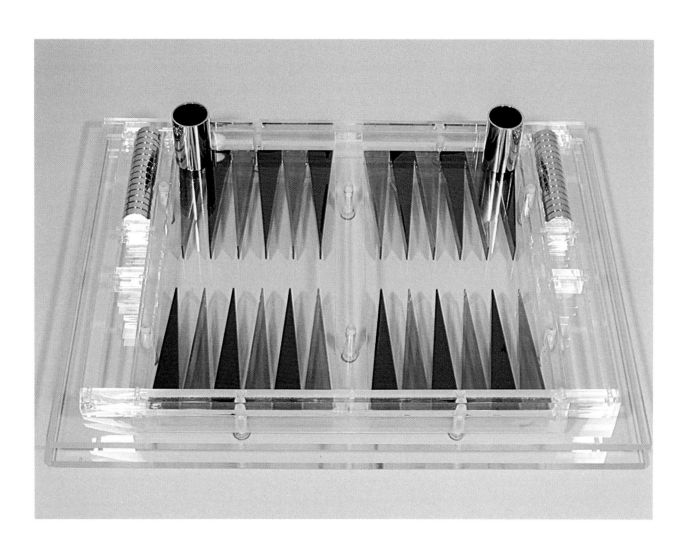

13   **Backgammon Set**   *1975*   *Lucite, gold and chrome*   *24" (square)*
Mr. and Mrs. Gerald Miller, Washington, D.C.

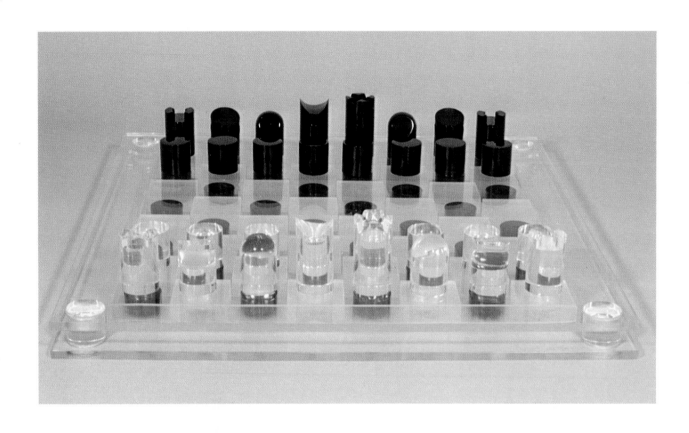

14   Chess Set   *1969   Lucite   30" (square)*

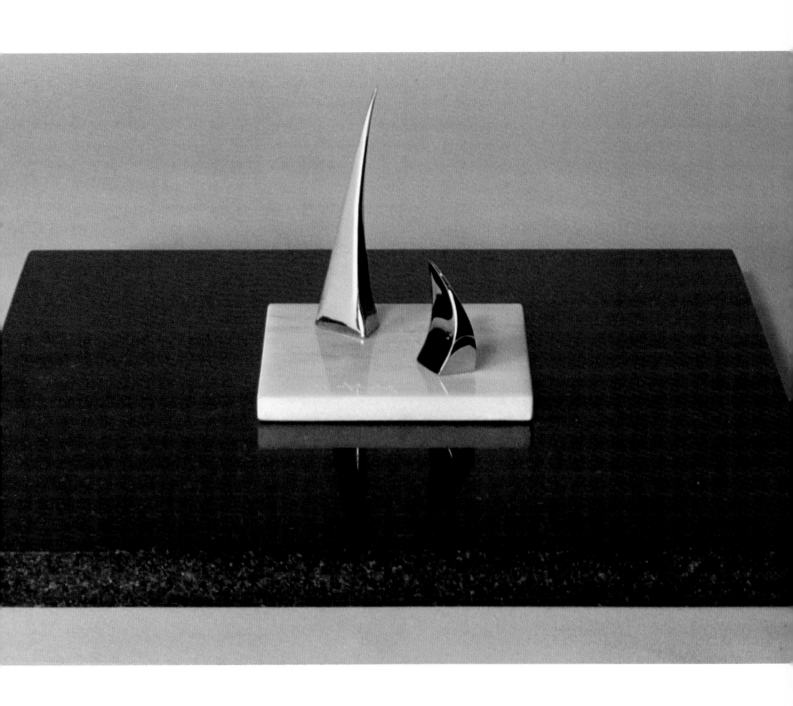

15   Tango   *1978*   *Steel and marble*   *4″*

16   Linkage   *1981   Bronze and granite   9"*

17   Siege   *1981   Bronze and granite   13"*

18   Déjà Vu   *1977   Lucite   8"*

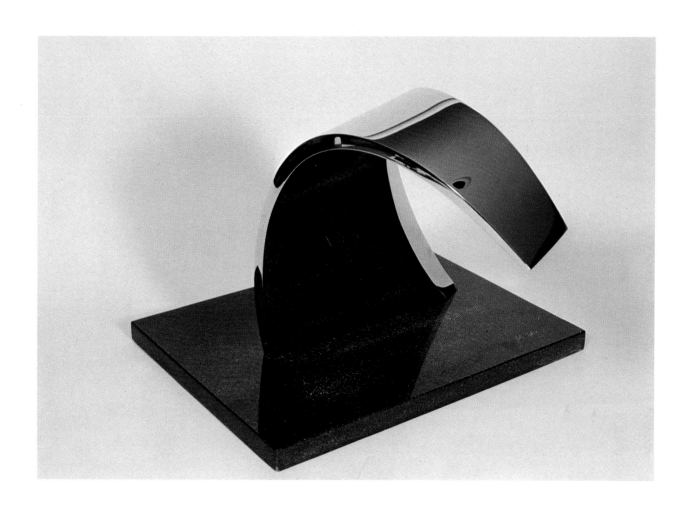

The flame-like pieces constitute another major body of work within John Safer's total output. The constructivist pieces came naturally from the nature of the material. The "flames" come naturally out of another property of Lucite; it softens when heated and can then be shaped.

A minor feature of Safer's undergraduate education was that in the laboratory he did from time to time fashion or modify glass vessels and instruments for himself and some of his fellow students. The activity was largely utilitarian convenience. But it did expose the student to the task of making a hard and brittle substance soft and malleable, with the goal of changing its shape. In the process of becoming a sculptor, John Safer applied this procedure in the first instance to those swizzle sticks, then to the rods of acrylic, the Lucite. The results were, initially, the twist pieces (Pl. 1, 2, & 3) here reproduced and others like them. In that work, the distinguishing note was that the essential form of the Lucite rod was never changed. The rod was turned and bent, even, literally, tied into knots, but it remained a rod.

There is, therefore, a fundamental material-handling change in the large group of Safer pieces called "flame-like." From that follows, naturally, a change in the look of the pieces and from that, a change in their significance, their resonance within the mind of the viewer. The change in look is from geometric and architectural to curving fluidity. The sinuosity of the twists is here carried a step further. If the twists suggest a conspiratorial interweaving of lines of power, the flame pieces suggest serpents menacing, plants growing, or blazes flickering. They suggest the organic rather than the mechanical. If John Safer's constructivist works stand as emblems for the shells we build to live and work within, the flame pieces portray the vulnerable but growing and endlessly potential human psyche within the shells, the psyche that, after all, constructs the shells in the first place.

One work in particular suggests a kind of link between these two major streams in Safer's sculpture. It is *CINQUANTAINE* (Pl. 21), a sculpture made as a birthday present, the sort of present only an artist or a good cook can give, although the artist's presents last longer. Two friends of the artist were celebrating their 50th birthdays together. The piece was made as a joint gift, to be shared 50–50. The title itself is a subtle deference to the widely accepted American convention that people are not to be asked to state their exact age. *Cinquantaine* does not mean "50." The word for 50 is *cinquant,* and that for fiftieth is *cinquantième. Cinquantaine* means "about 50," what we call "fiftyish." It's a nice touch and an ironic one since the date of the work permanently dates the recipients.

The piece itself flares up from its narrow root, expanding to its maximum lateral dimension at the double base of the two pyramids of which it consists. If a "fiftyish" person were feeling depressed about his advanced and advancing years, *CINQUANTAINE* would cheer him with its elegant thrust upward, its implication of Browning's promise that "the best is yet to be." For that, surely, is the interpretation of such a double form with such a title on such a double occasion. The linear boundaries of the work, both the verticals and the laterals or lateral-diagonals, link it with the constructivist pieces. The graceful curve that tops it off pledges its allegiance to the flames of the sculptor.

Two works considered together show an important development from one to the other, within the perceived similarity. *CRYSTAL* (Pl. 22) both in its title and its form remind us at once of the sculptor's undergraduate experience in working glass. The Lucite is beautifully formed out of the fire, bringing with it something of the shape fire itself assumes, at the same time implying hands joined and raised in supplication, thanksgiving, celebration. The enclosed space that adorns the top of *CRYSTAL* is elongated and split in *WRAITH* (Pl. 23). It is a very graceful form, as all of the flame works are in their different ways. The double gap that appears in the piece and even more strikingly in its shadow, is a leitmotif that recurs in Safer's work in this category, appearing variously as the life sign of the double helix, the "Möbius strip", a surface with a single side, or the mathematical symbol for infinity. All of these aspects of the form, singly and in combination, underlie its appearances in Safer's flame pieces.

Meanwhile, the slightly larger than life size of *WRAITH,* just over seven feet, helps explain the title. A wraith is an apparition of a person seen as mist or vapor, hence elongated but de-substantiated at the same time. The work embodies, or disembodies, that idea perfectly and is somehow, at once an imposing but diffident presence.

NIGHT FLIGHT (Pl. 24) incorporates a bronze glow into the Lucite torque of the work, which like *WRAITH* stands about seven feet high. The piece summons up the age of flight. It reminds us of those frail machines poised against the infinity of air space in what may be called the heroic period of aviation. Antoine de Saint-Exupéry was a French aviator of that period. Born with the century, he died in 1945. His best-known book was the allegorical *The Little Prince,* but for many his best book was *Night Flight,* in which, with none of the artificial encumbrances of allegory, the mysticism as well as the heroism of pioneer aviation is conveyed. With its implied reference to Saint-Exupéry, *NIGHT FLIGHT* is appropriately chaste and direct, with that suggestion of a soaring curve that recurs throughout the work of John Safer.

MISTRAL (Pl. 25) in bronze toned Lucite on an aluminum base, lends a touch of definition to a medium and form which, together, tend toward the dissolution of definition in the reflected and refracted light on, through, and inside the transparent curves. Five feet high, *MISTRAL* weaves before us, held in the firm but restrained grip of its controlled boundaries. The mistral is that strong, cold, seasonal wind of southern France thought, by long tradition, to affect the behavior of those too long exposed to it. There is, thus, an element of magic and the suggestion of change from the accustomed, implications subtly present in the power of *MISTRAL's* curves.

QUEST (Pl. 26) is in stainless steel and stands 5'8". Basically it combines the two different strains of *NIGHT FLIGHT* and *MISTRAL* in an upward sweep of turning, reflecting grace. The combination of form and material makes *QUEST* an outstanding example of the flame sculptures, with special reference to Walter Pater's statement of the eternal goal; "to burn always with this hard, gem-like flame, to maintain this ecstacy, is success in life." In ordinary human experience, ecstasy maintained is a contradiction in terms, but it is a condition of successful art and a condition attained in piece after piece of Safer's flame sculptures.

The flame-like form of *QUEST* combines a remarkable strength and grace. That combination is held to be a desirable goal of art in philosophic discourses from the Greeks through the New Testament to our entire poetic heritage. A form achieving goals so stated is inherently fundamental to the human condition.

SERPENTINE (Pl. 27) of bronze toned Lucite like *MISTRAL,* handles the flame motif in a unique manner. Rather than blazing upward, it coils sinuously. The title is well chosen: throughout Central and West Africa, the serpent is a powerful totemic force. The snake often appears carved in doors or coiled around staffs or posts, but occasionally the serpent is made into an independent, free-standing sculpture.

The serpent plays a vital role in Judaeo-Christian and Graeco-Roman mythology— in one the occasion of humanity's fall from grace, in the other the bearer or witness of Sibylline utterances—yet neither tradition includes much notable art embodying that intrinsically graceful form. Perhaps significantly, Safer's sculptural inspiration, Michelangelo, on the Sistine Ceiling, did portray the serpent erect.

The serpentine motif takes an entirely different form in *ASCENT,* (Pl. 28) like many of John Safer's works a maquette for a monumental sculpture. The rising, uncoiling, serpentine form is designed to be placed in a pool, so the maquette is placed in a shallow, circular area filled with water. Again, the combination is Lucite and aluminum, but this time with a difference. In most of the sculptures wherein Safer has combined the two materials, the sculpture is of Lucite and the base of aluminum. Here the positions are reversed. The aluminum sculpture, using the materials embodied in the machines of flight, ascends in space as it coils and cuts through time. *ASCENT* is one of the most unique, and one of the best of the artist's monumental works.

Even in its relatively diminutive size, eighteen inches high, *ASCENT* is a lovely thing, original among abstract sculpture, and yet a natural, inevitable form, embodying its symbolic goal: effortlessly, flight rises into the air, steadily accelerating as the angle increases.

PROBE (Pl. 29) is a small (ten inches-high) very simple work. But it was the first. That is the special meaning of the title *PROBE* within the body of John Safer's work. This was the first of the flame-like pieces, the sculptor's first effort to lay hands, literally, upon his chosen material and, like Omar, reshape it nearer to the heart's desire. With this stroke he made himself much more completely master of his material, and at the same time made the medium much more intimately part of the message. McLuhan may not have had art in mind, but from the caves of Lascaux onward, all artists have known that the relationship is inexorable. With *PROBE* Safer enormously expanded his artistic vocabulary and potential, and opened an unending series of doors.

INTERPLAY III (Pl. 30) in Lucite and brass implies growth and relationships. The defined edges of the ascending Lucite develop the feeling of life emerging from non-life that is the essence of this work. The piece rises in two trunks or stalks from out of the heavy metal. The two members cross, turn, confront or address each other, one higher, one lower. They could be lovers or blossoms emerging. Actually they are two vertical, shaped and curved columns of transparent, reflective and refractive substance in a relationship that changes constantly, harmoniously and sequentially as the viewer's eye moves about the piece.

28   In *ARTS* Magazine for June, 1978, C. Douglas Lewis, curator of sculpture at the National Gallery of Art, Washington, wrote, "The masterpiece of this emerging columnar-crystalline genre may have been Safer's great *FLAMBERGE* of 1971, a splendidly sinuous clear acrylic spiral flaring upward with a boldly-carved quadrilateral section to explode the ambient light into gem-like radiance at breath-taking scale." The description is impeccable. The piece certainly is a masterpiece, summing up solidly and succinctly a great deal that is tentative or implicit in earlier works. *FLAMBERGE* (Pl. 31) reads up and down and inside out with its lambent legibility. It is the supreme expression of its genre. The proportions and the light effects are so exquisitely correct that to be in its presence is to be content.

Flamberge is French for sword, although the French have so many other words for sword that this one is rarely used. The word means sword because it was the name of the weapon of the great legendary hero, Roland, Charlemagne's captain who, in the legend, beat back the dread Saracens at Roncesvalles, a pass in the Pyrenees.

One of the few uses in French of the name *Flamberge* for sword is in the phrase for drawing a sword, *Mettre flamberge au vent,* literally, to put one's sword in the wind. *FLAMBERGE* as sculpture has the same evocative quality and, etymology aside, the sculpture certainly implies a sword of flame.

If *FLAMBERGE* is the supreme expression to date of what Lewis descriptively calls the "columnar-crystalline genre," then *LIMITS OF INFINITY III* (Pl. 32) is the apotheosis of that form. Publicly placed in Washington, the large work—fifteen feet high—sits, stands, rests, breathes, is simply *there,* in the plaza of the building at 1101 Connecticut Avenue, a neighborhood of offices, restaurants, the Mayflower Hotel, boutiques and St. Matthew's Cathedral, the only one of the group professionally concerned with infinity.

The form in the center of the piece is somewhat simpler than that of *FLAMBERGE.* It should be: it is a segment of a larger arrangement. That turned form of bronze hangs within its bronze enclosure as if floating in space. It is, the shape reminds us, the symbol of infinity. The title, *LIMITS OF INFINITY,* is of course, a deliberate contradiction in terms. Contradiction or not, there is the infinity symbol afloat in the light and darkness, and there are the limits, the ovoid line around that twist of bronze. The granite block, which is not merely a suitable resting place but a vital part of the sculpture, brings the solid and finite earth into the equation. That block of stone is *our* base from which to contemplate infinity.

Seen from within the building at night, *LIMITS OF INFINITY* seems to hang, lighted itself, against a starry night. Seen from the outside, the piece announces the presence of an extraterrestrial force serenely arrived, as, by definition, infinity is.

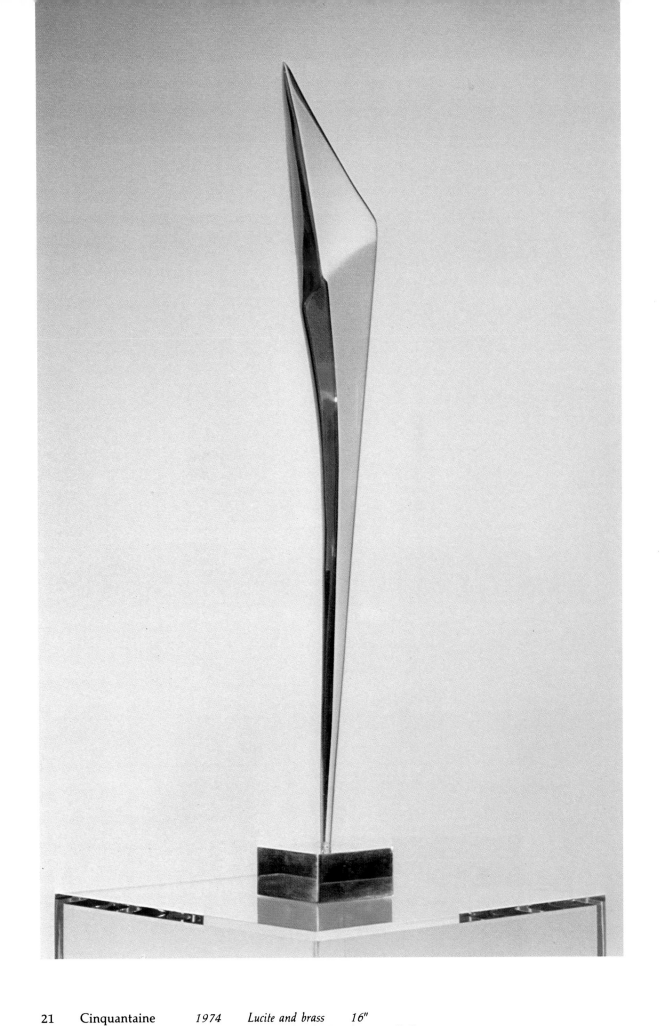

21   Cinquantaine   *1974*   *Lucite and brass*   *16"*
Mr. Arthur K. Mason and Mr. E. F. Brylawski, Washington, D.C.

22   Crystal   *1970*   *Lucite*   *29"*   *Mr. and Mrs. Robert Rosenthal, Washington, D.C.*

23   Wraith   *1978*   *Lucite and brass*   *85"*

▶

24   Night Flight   *1974*   *Lucite and brass*   *85"*

25   Mistral   *1980*   *Lucite and aluminum*   *58"*

▶

27   Serpentine   *1980*   *Lucite and aluminum*   *53"*

◀ 26   Quest   *1979*   *Steel and granite*   *68"*
Milwaukee Art Museum, Milwaukee, Wisconsin   *Mr. and Mrs. Stuart Bernstein, Washington, D.C.*

▶

31   Flamberge   *1971*   *Lucite and brass*   *30"*   *Mrs. S. P. Fagadau, Dallas, Texas*

◀ 30   Interplay III   *1973*   *Lucite and brass*   *51"*   *Mr. and Mrs. J. J. Kahn, Bethesda, Md.*

32   Limits of Infinity III   *1979*   *Bronze and granite*   *180"*   *Mr. and Mrs. Gerald Miller*
On display in front of 1101 Connecticut Ave., Washington, D.C.   ▶

Inevitably, the flame pieces merge into a similar but distinctly different group of Safer's works, those which have an anthropoid quality, and that includes, in several cases, animals as well as men. Flames become people. That happens in Dante and in Blake. It is a defensible position that the essence of El Greco is the interchangeability of flames and people, the upward, spiritual attentuation of the people turning into flame, the gravitational forces acting on the flames, transforming them into people.

That process seems to define *SOLILOQUY* (Pl. 33), seven feet high in stainless steel. In the flame pieces, the essential movement of the work would be the same, a strong sweep upward. Here, however, the sweep becomes a little more angular: fluid fire develops elbows and shoulders and veers toward the human. The steel surface echoes, however distantly, the armor of El Greco's grandees. Flame coalesces into the armored spirit. In the end, however, the essence that remains has a minor dissonance that implies a haunting beauty. It is this that remains long after the viewer has turned away from this work.

NULL SPACE (Pls. 34 & 35) is one of several of Safer's ideas he has executed in different media; here it is shown in Lucite with a brass base, and also in the classic sculptural bronze. The height of both is the same, three and a half feet. The configuration is the same: up from the base to a seemingly precarious balance, a swelling out to contained space, another steep rise through a narrower passage into a rapid termination. The bronze, again, is armor, reflecting light out in self-defense. The Lucite is more like flesh and mind, letting light in for its own sake and letting its reverberations charm and illumine.

The title raises conundrum-like questions, is space a void, or does it have inherent positive qualities? The two elegant figures refuse all but tentative answers.

LAOCOÖN REVISITED (Pl. 36) lifesize in Lucite on an aluminum base, is, intentionally or not, an homage from the sculptor to the guiding spirit of the greatest sculptor of the past. Michelangelo captured the young lieutenant's heart and spirit in Rome and Florence almost 400 years after the older sculptor's death. The *Laocoön* was to Michelangelo's generation what Michelangelo himself was to the young Safer. When the antique statue of the Trojan priest, who warned against the Greeks bearing gifts, was unearthed, Rome, then

Italy, then Europe, were successively astounded at the twisting, intertwining limbs and muscles and serpents, all poised each against the other. Safer's piece is an act of artistic piety, as, in its way, Michelangelo's *Pièta* was an act of religious piety.

SAMURAI (Pl. 37), five feet high in Lucite on brass, once again speaks in muted dissonances. As with so many of John Safer's sculptures, this is no attempt to portray a Samurai warrior in a specific representative sense. Rather, this is a work which from one view, is an arrangement of curves and planes in space. Yet, those curves and planes imply something of the strength and discipline symbolized by the code of the Samurai. The completed entity as perceived by the outside eye blends the pure abstraction with the qualities implied in the title to achieve something a little beyond that which either might accomplish separately.

LOGOS (Pl. 38) is by name the quintessential union of spirit and matter to which an artist can aspire. In the Greek, "logos" is the key word of the first, awe-inspiring sentence of the Gospel According to St. John: "In the beginning was the Word (Logos) and the Word was made flesh and dwelt amongst us." This awe-inspiring figure in Lucite on brass embodies the idea, en-fleshes the Word.

In the midst of such soaring ideas in the art of John Safer, it is reassuring, comforting, even rather endearing, to come across two works which express, instead, a familial intimacy, an enjoyable affection. The works are *CLOVIS* (Pl. 39), and *JANINE* (Pl. 40). Janine is John Safer's daughter. Clovis is more complex, nomenclaturally. In the immediate instance, it is the name of Janine's cat. That's why the two pieces go together. But there is more to Clovis than that. The first time the name appears in history, it is as the first king of the Franks, who tried to seize control of what is now France after the fall of Rome.

The second Clovis in literature and the one for whom Janine's cat was directly named was the terribly precious, but somehow endearing young man in the works of "Saki". There is thus majesty and irony, a rare combination, lurking in the background, and both inherent in this work. The cat form goes back to Egypt in its majesty, then to China to descend from the throne. Here as in many of his sculptures, Safer did not set out to create a portrait of a cat but rather, having set out to carve a satisfying figure of a certain complexity, recognized in the finished work a correspondence with something in his experience.

That's true, also, of *JANINE.* To quote the artist "I had created a simple, graceful figure, and in naming it, wanted to associate it with someone who, more than anyone else, had added grace, harmony and happiness to my life."

34   Null Space   *1979*   *Bronze*   *42"*   *Mr. and Mrs. Steven Winkelman, Bethesda, Md.*

33   Soliloquy   *1980*   *Steel*   *83"*
◀   *Mr. and Mrs. Charles Lubar, London, England*   *Mr. and Mrs. Bruce Winston, Potomac, Maryland*

35   Null Space   *1979*   *Lucite and brass*   *42"*

38   Logos   *1976   Lucite and brass   18"*

◀ 37   Samurai   *1974   Lucite   61"   On display—State Department, Washington, D.C.*

◀ ◀   36   Laocoön Revisited   *1975   Lucite and aluminum   69"*

39   Clovis   *1974*   *Lucite and brass*   *24"*

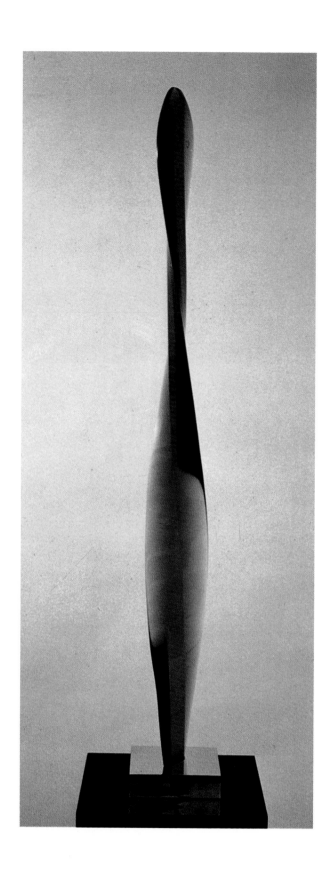

40   Janine   *1971   Lucite and brass   28"*

Since the most popular subject of sculpture by far, through the centuries, is the human figure and since the human in art tends to be shown standing more often than sitting, let alone lying down, it follows that sculpture traditionally is more vertical than horizontal. That's also true of John Safer's work, but he has created a few horizontal pieces of striking interest.

This is reasonable when you recall that the art which had the greatest impact on the young Safer's developing ideas about art was that of Michelangelo in Rome and Florence. In the latter city repose four of the greatest sculptures of the reclining figure ever made, Michelangelo's Times of Day that adorn the Medici tombs in the crypt of the New Sacristy.

Safer's horizontal pieces are completely different, not merely in being abstract as opposed to figurative, but more fundamentally in having none of the agony and angst of those unforgettable figures in Florence. Generally speaking, Safer aims for and achieves serenity in his sculpture and this is never truer than in the few works that are horizontal in format.

PLAINT (Pl. 41), the smallest of the group, illustrates the point. Despite the title, which refers to a lamentation, this piece at first suggests, perhaps, an abstract bird completely at rest. Seen in terms of the title, it is a gently rising sonority, brief in duration, more like a shaped and ordered Gregorian chant than a deeply felt emotional protest against the sorrows and troubles of life. Serenity has been achieved. Incidentally, this piece was purchased by members of the American Foreign Service as a wedding gift for the Secretary of State. Whether the stress should be on the serenity or on the plaint is a good question.

ARIEL (Pl. 42) suggests flight in the name and in the form. This is a bird taking off or landing, poised, wings spread. The brass standard holds the Lucite like a launcher. Ariel, of course, was the spirit servant to the magician Prospero in *The Tempest*. His opening announcement lists his abilities: "to fly, to swim, to dive into the fire, to ride on the curl'd clouds." This Ariel looks fully capable of all those modes of travel. The serenity mentioned above is seen, too, in the very choice of Ariel as subject and not that spirit's opposite fellow-servant, Caliban. Appropriately, Ariel deals with the ultimate human misfortune, death, in his song "Full fathom five". But with its "sea-change" into the "rich and strange" the focus is shifted from death to transfiguration.

That same shift takes place in Safer's *PERSEPHONE* (Pl. 43), a larger Lucite work, 40" × 22". In Greek myth, Persephone was the daughter of Ceres, seized by Pluto, god of the underworld, and, finally, allowed for half of each year to leave Pluto and the darkness of the earth, to return to the sunshine of spring and summer. The story of Persephone is, of course, one of the basic stories of death and transfiguration and from time immemorial has been received as an allegory of farming: the seed thrown into the dark earth to reappear later as golden grain.

Safer's *PERSEPHONE* rises from out of the dark earth. That emerging figure expresses the rebirth of the year, of life and its sustenance. Finally, it is one of those "perfect" shapes that Safer has a predeliction for in his work, sometimes those handed down from generation to generation, like the cube and the sphere, sometimes an original shape, apparently arrived at simply by instinct. Whichever it is, Safer's figures are clean and complete and to look at them is to feel in harmony with the environment.

The most horizontal of the horizontal works are the two *PISCES* pieces (Pls. 44 & 45), but their horizontality has nothing in it at all of the supine, the slack, the sleeping. Smooth, sleek, images of graceful power, both of these bronze fish show the influence on his use of that medium of Safer's earlier and continuing use of acrylic. They are shaped, planed, curved to suggest forceful ease of movement. Their gleaming surfaces have something of the reflected light the underwater swimmer sees along the forms of fish passing at a distance.

From a Zodiacal point of view, it is good that there are two of these piscatorial pieces, for their mythical predecessors came into the starry heavens and thence into the consciousness of the astrologically minded as a pair, and a divine pair at that: the two fish are Aphrodite and Eros, the goddess and the god of love. There is something of Eros in these bronze forms thrusting forward without threat but imbued with purpose. But, again, the principal thrust is completeness, purity, and universality.

As a boy who missed most normal athletic play by reason of age dislocation in school, John Safer has made up for it and still does. Among the enthusiasms and joys of his life are the games of golf and tennis. He plays and has played quite a bit of tournament golf. Like his predecessors in sculpture from the Greeks to the Renaissance, he has been fascinated by the beauty implicit in the movements of the trained athlete. It is not surprising that he has used both games as subjects for sculpture. Considering the quality of his work, it is not surprising that one of his pieces in the field of each sport has become an official trophy of international standing. And it is not surprising at all that the works should have emerged, not diminutive bronze replicas of Bobby Jones or Bill Tilden, but rather direct, persuasive and powerful portraits of what it must have felt like to be Jones or Tilden at their supreme moments of exertion and exhilaration.

Golf resembles chess in that there is a long time between shots. But golf has its supreme moments of power and motion. One of those moments is the swing and that is the moment immortalized in the golf *TROPHY* (Pl. 46).

Made of bronze and standing four feet high, the piece is the embodiment of the perfect stroke, yet there is no anthropomorphizing of the golfer. The golfer, in fact, is so stylized he is represented only by a slab, similar to the central element of *BAUHAUS REMEMBERED.* Attached at only one point to its column is the bronze form that is not so much a circle as an extended arc. The edge from pillar to circumference, suggesting abstractly accelerating rotation, narrows rapidly as the eye follows the curve. The bronze sheet continues on its course and contracts almost to a point as it approaches and fuses with the outside curve.

In classic art criticism, as developed by Heinrich Wölfflin and, later by Bernard Berenson, there is a notion of the kinetic effect: even though the painting or the sculpture is obviously standing still, the sensitive viewer feels movement, the dynamic relationships of weights and forces in the work. The idea has rarely been better embodied than in the golf *TROPHY.*

The tennis *TROPHY* (Pl. 47) approaches the problem of motion in a slightly less abstract manner. In bronze on a granite base, the tennis trophy consists of two arcs meeting at a single point. They convey the idea of the action and flow of the athlete totally at one with himself and his sport. Both segments of the sculpture are curved, supple, in motion, dynamic. The game is on. In the golf piece, the vertical member is stationary, it is the fulcrum about which the swing revolves.

The difference is one of the two games. Tennis does not have long waiting periods between shots. Every moment demands alertness. Every shot immediately creates the expectation of its return. That's what is conveyed by this piece. The vertical, supporting member is not just in support. It's in action, tense, alert. Its multiple curves suggest the flow and ease of the athlete. With all of the movement and tension, this sculpture, as a totality, resolves those dynamics leaving the viewer with a feeling of balance and harmony. This is an outstanding sculpture.

Safer's sculptor mentor, Michelangelo, created, as the center-pieces of those horizontal figures surmounting the Medici tombs, the two effigies of the two very minor Medici there interred. The two seated figures have always been accepted as the master's interpretations of "The Active Life" and "The Contemplative Life".

If the tennis and golf trophies can reasonably be interpreted as John Safer's sculptural embodiments of "The Active Life," *CHANDELLE* (Pl. 48) can be seen as a superb expression of "The Contemplative Life". Just under six feet high, *CHANDELLE* is almost equally divided between the pointed oval form of the top and the base-pedestal of the bottom, though, perhaps, this is not self evident. There is a bit of sculptural skill at the base that seems to separate the ovoid shape from the pedestal and at the same time to make the pedestal appear longer, an effect partially achieved by having the ovoid open, the pedestal closed and solid.

As the name implies, *CHANDELLE* comes out of the "flame" series of Safer's sculptures; the word is French for candle; the flame is rounded and closed.

35

After hacking through centuries of jungle growth into the ruins of an ancient temple lighted by the sun streaming through a hole in the roof, it would not be surprising to find this shape in the center of that natural spotlight. The arcane quality of that arch does not yield to the mathematical analysis applicable to the arches of the Roman, Romanesque, Gothic or Renaissance eras. Here we sense that the mathematics are present but invisible, complex. The form is simply there, ineluctable, ineffable, eternal.

A late starter in sculpture, John Safer has moved fast, not because of the sense of time lost, but rather because of the experience, feeling and understanding that he had amassed before coming to sculpture.

Attracted to the new material Lucite, with its remarkable qualities, Safer quickly made himself master of that medium; he mastered, too, the tools that enabled him to cut, shape, warp, mould, anneal, smooth and shine. He developed many new techniques of his own and with them a new vision. He then brought these new techniques and new approaches to traditional sculptural materials. He synthesized the old and the new in a manner totally his own.

A child of his century, he worked in his century's two great sculptural modes of constructivism and biomorphism, things made and things grown in life. His vision combined the things that could be done in the old materials and the approaches he had found for the new. Bringing these concepts together, he created sculptures which give us a new vision of ourselves and our universe.

He can be intimate, endearing, classical in turn. The great gift so far not totally realized is monumentality. He grew up in a city of monuments and quite rightly rejected most of them. None the less, he developed a remarkable sense of the monumental. John Safer has the ability to embody monumental concepts in sculptures, regardless of size, a gift he shares with Moore, Lipchitz, and Cellini.

Assuredly, the opportunity will come to develop John Safer's monumental potential. In the meantime, Safer's sure hand will contribute to the artistic redemption of an end of the century period often deplored for its sterility.

Translating ideas into elegant forms, manipulating geometry into monuments, discovering forms that speak mysteriously to us all of values and proportions that are forever, John Safer brings grace and thought to a time in art which is our own.

36

41   Plaint   *1974   Lucite and brass   12"*   *Mr. and Mrs. Henry Kissinger, Washington, D.C.*

42   Ariel   *1977   Lucite and brass   12" x 26"*

43   Persephone   *1979   Lucite   22" x 40"*

44   Pisces III   *1974   Bronze and marble   6" x 23"   Mr. Caio Machado, Rio de Janeiro, Brazil*

45   Pisces IV   *1975   Bronze   6" x 23"*
Mr. and Mrs. Seymour Fain, Washington, D.C.   Mr. C. Douglas Lewis, Washington, D.C.

46   Trophy (Golf)   *1977*   *Bronze*   *48"*   *World Series of Golf, Firestone Country Club, Akron, Ohio*

47   Trophy (Tennis)   *1982   Bronze and granite   74"   D.C. National Bank Tennis Classic Trophy*
On display at D.C. National Bank, 1801K St., N.W., Washington, D.C.

48   Chandelle   *1969*   *Lucite*   *71"*   *Mrs. June Degnan, San Francisco, California*